The Illustrated Guide
to
Free Hugs

Written by Juan Mann

Illustrations by Krista Brennan

Digital edition first published 2008

This edition published 2010

JUAN MANN

To the heroes who helped make me.

To the villains who tried to break me.

I dedicate this book to the one woman who keeps encouraging and supporting me to be every bit the man I have become.

Mee Yeon, I love you.

KRISTA BRENNAN

Inspiration, support, love, generosity; everything this book celebrates, I learned from my bright-eyed hero, Mitch.

Jüan   Krista

"There is no love in fear."
~ *Maynard James Keenan*

"Be kind; everyone you meet is fighting a hard battle."
~ *Plato*

"There are no strangers here; only friends you haven't yet met."
~ *William Butler Yeats*

Free

1. Without cost, payment, or charge;
2. Given without consideration of a return or reward;
3. Not subject to special regulations, restrictions, duties, etc;
4. Acting without self-restraint or reserve;
5. Ready or generous in giving;
6. That may be used by or is open to all;

Hugs

1. To clasp or hold closely, especially in one's arms; embrace or enfold, as in affection;
2. To keep very close;
3. An affectionate embrace.

From Scandinavian/Old Norse *hugga*, to comfort, console

Campaign

1. A series of actions energetically pursued to advance a principle or tending toward a particular end;
2. To exert oneself continuously, vigorously, or obtrusively to gain an end or be an advocate for a certain cause.

Free Hugs Campaign

1. To offer everyone and anyone an embrace, free of charge, until such time as nobody partakes of the unlimited offer.

Definitions from Google.com

WHAT IS FREE HUGS ALL ABOUT?

Free Hugs is an international kindness initiative based on the simple idea of offering hugs to complete strangers.

The first Free Hugs were offered on Wednesday June 30th, 2004 in an effort to cheer up just one person's day.

Mine.

Offering Free Hugs has many purposes. From making someone's day a little brighter to meeting new people and showing the world that strangers aren't so bad after all. It's also about bringing people together and sharing a happy moment before heading back out into the world feeling a little happier about themselves.

Free Hugs is all about people being there for each other.

When you're feeling sad and alone in the world, it helps to talk to someone, to share a laugh, to see someone smile at you, to have somebody wrap their arms around you in a supportive embrace and reassure you that everything will be alright. But what about those people who don't have somebody? Whose families live far away? Whose friends just don't understand?

Once upon a time that sad and lonely person was me.

I RETURNED TO SYDNEY...

From London after my family fell apart, my fiancée left me and my life seemed in ruins. The last words my Dad shared with me before I went my own way had been, "You can't change the world, but you can make a difference."

Surely, I couldn't change the world. Without family or purpose, without a dream, a support or a kind shoulder to lean on, what difference could I make?

I spent months living alone in the Blue Mountains, having little contact with the people and the world around me.

Every day, I remembered that moment of despair, standing alone in the arrivals terminal at Sydney Airport. Watching other passengers meeting their waiting friends and family with open arms and smiling faces, happy to see each other again.

Even complete strangers had people with names on signs to meet them!

More than anything in the world, I wanted someone out there to be waiting for me. To be happy to see me, to smile at me, to throw their arms around me and tell me that everything would be alright.

I found it hard to relate to the world and the world found it hard to relate to me in my infinite self-pity. I only felt like I was a part of the world when I was stuck in traffic, staring at the same red traffic light as the person in the car beside me. Human contact became something that was limited to a cashier's hand brushing mine when returning my change in stores.

After a few months of solitude, an old friend tracked me down in the Blue Mountains. He called me up and invited me along to a party, to rejoin society as it were and find a little joy in the world. But I had nothing to offer anyone. Just sadness, sorrow and misery.

Standing in an empty corner of the party, watching people enjoying each other's company, I wondered, "I have nothing to talk about, I have no way of making someone else smile... what could I do to cheer somebody else up? What will I do to cheer up myself?"

While I was drowning myself in my thoughts a young lady strolled across this crowded room and right up to me, smiled into my eyes and wrapped her arms around me.

This young lady had been the first person to hug me in an eternity. My problems weren't solved, the world hadn't changed there and then, but that hug had made a difference to my life. I felt happier!

In that moment I discovered something I'd known all along, but hadn't realised or had simply forgotten in my sadness. I'd found the one thing I'd been truly missing, in all that time I'd spent alone.

Just a simple little hug.

I immediately knew what I was going to do.

I was going to make a sign and offer Free Hugs to everyone and anyone. It doesn't matter how rich or how poor, how old or how young, who they were or where they came from. A free hug would be free of charge and free for everyone in the world.

From Korea...

To France...

And Russia too...

There's a Free Hug waiting, just for you!

THE IMPORTANCE OF HUGS

Touch is one of the most important of our five senses. Without it we feel detached from the people around us. It is one of the first senses we develop in the womb. One of the most commonly accepted forms of touch among people is also one of the first experiences we have in the world.

A hug!

There is no better way to understand the importance of hugs than to be deprived of them. For those who have experienced a deprivation of human contact, you will know how important it feels to share a simple embrace.

In those dire moments of hug deprivation even one hug can be enough to cheer you up.

Research by US psychologists Karen Grewen and Karen Light has shown that when people hug, the brain releases the chemical oxytocin. This encourages social bonding, increases our willingness to trust and decreases fear. It has also shown that hugs are great for your heart. A study was conducted that measured the heart rates and blood pressure of two groups of people, a group of huggers and a group of non-huggers. Those who went without hugs were found to have a higher blood pressure and resting heart rate in comparison to the group of huggers, who had noticeably healthier results.

In 1995 a pair of prematurely born twins were being cared for in hospital. While one of the twins seemed quite healthy, her sister was suffering. After trying a range of medical approaches, the nurse on duty, Gayle Kasparian, placed the twins in bed together. The twins immediately snuggled up to each other. As one placed her arm around the other, the frail infant's health began to improve. You can never underestimate the power of a hug!

The need for hugs doesn't disappear as we grow older, though it seems we are less willing to give them. Research on people of all ages has proven that a hug is essential for physical and emotional well-being.

Without hugs we can become sad, withdrawn and depressed. A hug provides solace, safety and tenderness. A hug provides us with social contact, an overall sense of wellbeing and a feeling of importance and belonging.

With a Free Hugs sign or shirt, no matter who you are or where you may find yourself in the world, you'll never experience the horrors of hug deprivation again!

My First Free Hugs sign...

Took me two nights to make. When people looked at it, I wanted them to realise I was serious. To take notice of what I was offering and not just dismiss it as some young man playing a prank or just another viral marketing campaign.

I'd spent the days before my first Free Hugs day walking around the city looking for the busiest places. I was searching for outdoor areas that had plenty of shade and plenty of people walking by. I had a short-list of places to go. The harbour side at Circular Quay was full of tourists and had beautiful views of the Harbour Bridge and Opera House. Martin Place was full of business people during lunch hour, rushing about their day. The Pitt Street Mall had tourists, business people and locals.

It was perfect. Well, perfect for what I was going to do.

Everything was covered. I had my location. I had my sign offering Free Hugs and I had a bright red Hawaiian shirt that I'd painted "Juan Mann – One Love" on the back.

People might not take me seriously or even take me up on the offer of a free hug, but they just might smile and that would be enough.

I'd prepared everything I could have before the day. The only thing I couldn't prepare in advance was the courage to carry through with what I'd planned. I knew what I had to do.

I wasn't going to let my fear hold me back.

THE DIFFERENT TYPES OF HUGS

Do you hug your friends in the same way you hug your grandparents?

Do you hug the same way when you are celebrating as you do when you are sad?

There are different types of hugs, each one with a unique significance.

A bear hug means something different to a group hug. A group hug means something different to a cuddle, but they all have something in common.

They feel good and make you feel even better.

The Free Hugs I've given to strangers aren't the same as the hugs I've received from family and after sharing hundreds of thousands of hugs with people from all over the world, I've noticed a few things.

A hug consists of three separate parts. The position of each huggers bodies in relation to each other, the configuration of their arms around each other and the placement of their hands. Each element contributes to the delivery of an awesome hug.

But what makes such a perfect little embrace?

The perfect hug for me is a gentle cuddle with the over arm/under arm technique and a slight amount of back rubbing. The hug that suits you best could be completely different.

This is just a short selection of the types of hugs and their variations. Mix them up, mash them together and create your very own perfect embrace.

THE A-FRAME HUG

The "A" in the A-Frame Hug stands for awkward.

The A-Frame Hug gets it name from the shape that the two huggers' bodies make when seen from a distance.

An A-Frame Hug occurs when two people stand at a fixed distance, lean their heads in towards each other and wrap their arms around each other's shoulders. Except for heads on each others' shoulders and hands on each others' backs, the two bodies do not come into contact.

When offering Free Hugs, this may be the most common type of hug you receive from people who appreciate what you're doing.

After noticing people giving you an A-Frame Hug, you'll probably be amused. You'll think "This person is a little uncomfortable hugging me, but hey, it's nice enough that they made the effort." You'll be happy knowing that the person you've just hugged might have done something they never thought they could do.

An A-Frame Hug is like the opening hug in a relationship between two strangers. It's a great way of getting to know someone without overstepping their personal boundaries. It may seem a little awkward, but a hug is a personal thing and everyone's personal space is something to be respected.

Photo Opportunity Hug

The Photo Opportunity Hug is one for the world to see. It occurs when the hugger and huggee stand side by with their arms around each other and smile for a camera or any other audience.

Almost everyone who asks for a photo when you're offering Free Hugs, will give you a Photo Op Hug. Every time you've posed for a photo with a friend, a partner or a loved one, have you noticed how someone will slip their arm around somebody else, all for the camera? You've just copped the Photo Op Hug.

There is a variation of the Photo Op Hug that is common among couples, who walk with their arms around each other. This is an advanced form of hugging that shouldn't be attempted without training, practice and a skilled partner.

When a couple meets somebody in the street and they start walking, they might embrace like this. It creates a snapshot in the observer's mind that these people are a couple.

The Photo Op Hug when not performed in front of a camera can make you feel as though you and the person you're hugging belong together. There's a personal bond there that doesn't need a camera or an audience to re-affirm how special this hug is.

THE CUDDLE

A Cuddle requires a complete absence of space between two huggers. With their bodies pressed together and their arms thrown right around each other, if you haven't been cuddled, you simply haven't lived.

A cuddle is a firm yet forgiving hug and is a physical manifestation of publicly appropriate love between people. It can also be a great way to relax after a stressful experience.

The close physical proximity of the cuddlers is indicative of their shared trust and affection.

Parents cuddle their children, partners cuddle each other, close friends will offer each other a cuddle in times of happiness or need. A cuddle is the most intimate hug you can share.

People can cuddle everywhere and anywhere, couples cuddle together on the couch, parents cuddle their children before heading off to work or school, children cuddle their stuffed animals before sleeping at night.

It's easy to understand that a cuddle makes you feel loved. It can make you feel important to somebody and shows them that they mean something special to you.

A Cuddler is someone who makes you feel comfortable.

THE MAN HUG

A Man Hug is a fusion of a handshake and a hug. It opens with a handshake as the huggers lean towards each other. With their free hand they pat each other on the back vigorously, before separating quickly.

The handshake, held at waist height, prevents the chests of either hugger from coming into contact, though on occasion the men will bring their opposing shoulders into brief contact with each other.

Outside of a sporting victory or achievement, anywhere men-friends can be found hugging you'll find them sharing a Man Hug.

Men adopt this hug with other men in an effort to quite simply avoid "junk touching" without settling for a meagre handshake. It shows a willingness to share an embrace, but a fear of how people watching two grown men hugging it out will judge them.

That said, a man hug is an awesome embrace and one truly worthy of inclusion in this book and any self respecting hugger's repertoire of embraces. Find a man and man hug it out today!

THE LIFT AND SPIN HUG

The Lift and Spin Hug is an advanced hug, not for the beginner or the faint of heart. The hugger lifts the huggee off the ground and spins around in a circle before returning the huggee to the ground. Think of it as the merry-go-round of hugs!

The Lift and Spin Hug is one of the most spontaneous hugs and is both physically and emotionally uplifting for lovers, parents and sometimes complete strangers alike.

This is one of the fun of all embraces. It plants a smile on your face, places some laughter in your heart, a twinkle in your eye and puts a spark into life.

The Lift and Spin Hug is a memory maker.

The Run and Jump Hug

The Run and Jump Hug could also be called the Slow Motion Romantic Comedy Hug. You've seen this before, where the love interests in a film run towards each other and one leaps into the others arms. Remove the slow motion and the romantic comedy and you've got yourself the Run and Jump Hug.

Lovers use it to express their romance, children use it to be caught by their parents and sometimes complete strangers will run and leap into your open arms when you offer Free Hugs!

This kind of hug can be found on grassy fields, cinema screens, airport arrival halls, your city streets and anywhere people are pleased to see each other.

This may be one of the most exhilarating types of hug around. There's a thrill in seeing someone running towards you, with arms wide open and a smile on their face. In watching them leap into your arms. You may have seen it before, but to experience it for yourself is not something you will soon forget.

CAUTION

The Run and Jump Hug is not for the faint of heart!

THE KOALA HUG AKA SIDE ON HUG

The Koala Hug or Side On Hug looks a lot like a Koala clinging to a tree. One hugger stands side on to the other, their shoulder resting against the chest of the person hugging them, so their bodies form a sort of 'T' shape.

The Koala Hug requires a level of familiarity, comfort and expectation that strangers cannot provide.

When a huggee finds themselves caught up in a task, the hugger will approach from their side and wrap their arms around the shoulders or waist of the huggee. The Koala Hug tends to occur most regularly when the huggee's attention is drawn away to other tasks, sights or experiences.

A Koala Hugger always wants to share themselves with you.

THE SURPRISE HUG

The Surprise Hug can be given to anybody with their back turned, whether they're sitting, standing or kneeling.

A pair of arms snake around your waist and a face presses against your back. You look around, but can't see the person hugging you. Their hands disappear back as they step away. You turn around for the real surprise: to discover who it was that just hugged you!

People who give this hug are looking to affectionately surprise somebody, without recognition, without invitation and without excuse.

Wherever you find someone meeting up with a friend or wherever somebody is sitting, toiling away, someone who loves them may sneak up behind them for a quick Surprise Hug. A Surprise Hug isn't for people with any form of medical complaint or heart condition.

Arms' Length Hug

Two huggers hold each other's arms at the elbows while smiling into each other's eyes. This is an excellent way to maintain a close level of contact with somebody after hugging them, while continuing a conversation.

Similar to the A-Frame, this hug is also for those people who aren't quite comfortable sharing an embrace with somebody.

This variation of a hug is common between people who either have never met before, or people who are very familiar with each other. Used either as a method of holding someone at a distance, or as a method of keeping them close to you while talking. Its meaning is varied though the intention is clear depending on the context of the embrace.

If used as a method of keeping someone at a distance, this hug leaves you with the knowledge of the other person's physical boundaries. As a method of keeping someone close while continuing a conversation, it leaves you feeling wanted...or trapped.

An At Arms' Length Hugger doesn't want you to leave... or get any closer.

THE GROUP HUG

A Group Hug is a life affirming experience. Think of a riot. Now imagine the happy alternative, a group of people piled together, with arms around each other and laughter in the air. A Group Hug is a free form, free for all, hug for three or more people. The more the merrier!

A Huddle is a form of group hug, more for the purpose of communicating a message amongst people and less as a method of showing someone you care. That said, huddles can become group hugs in two easy steps. Step One, throw your arms around the person beside you. Step Two, yell out "Group Hug!" Step Three, embrace.

Teams celebrating a victory, groups commemorating a happy moment, families, friends piling together for a photo and gatherings of more than three people will almost always end in a group hug.

A Group Hug leaves you feeling like a part of something amazing, with the knowledge that you're surrounded by some awesome people.

THE BEAR HUG

A Bear Hug involves the hugger grabbing the huggee around the arms and squeezing them as tightly as possible. Sometimes, the enthusiasm of the bear hugger can lift the huggee right off the ground, hopefully without cracking any ribs.

A Bear Hug is delivered by anyone who has the strength to give it. Uncles will almost always bear hug their nieces and nephews, children will always bear hug their stuffed animals but bears should never, ever be hugged by people. They get cranky.

A Bear Hug can make you feel like your lungs will burst and your head might pop right off, but most of all a Bear Hug makes you feel special. Nobody puts that much effort into a hug unless they really mean it!

If you're the person receiving a Bear Hug, you get to rest safe in the knowledge that you survived this one until the next time somebody tries to hug the life out of you. If someone can deliver a good proper Bear Hug, then you're in safe arms...once you've escaped the embrace.

A Bear Hug can be one of the most comforting hugs of all. It tells you that the person hugging you can keep you safe and watch over you.

A Bear Hugger is a protector.

ACROSS THE THRESHOLD HUG

One hugger leaps into the waiting arms of the huggee and wraps their arms around their neck or shoulders. The huggee carries the hugger in the same fashion as a newly-wed couple.

It's a traditional style of hug and rarely seen outside of such a joyous context. An Across the Threshold Hug given outside of such a traditional setting will still give those viewing the embrace an impression of a recently married couple.

Couples initiate this type of hug anywhere. At a family gathering an Across the Threshold Hug will have family members calling for a wedding.

THE ARM HUG

One hugger latches onto the arm of another person, hugging their arm instead of the whole body.

The Arm Hug is most commonly used by children or partners in an effort to grab attention in order to share something the hugger has found interesting. People will also use this type of hug in an attempt to keep up with their hugging target.

The Arm Hug is native to environments such as shopping malls, supermarkets, playgrounds, festivals and events - anywhere you'll find somebody trying to hold onto another person, or to keep up with them in a busy crowd.

Once initiated, an arm hug often shifts into a photo opportunity or koala hug, as the huggee more fully embraces the hugger.

An Arm Hugger will follow in your footsteps.

ARM APPROACHES AND HANDY VARIATIONS

Now that we have covered the basic style of hug, we can look at some other techniques, approaches and variations on a hug.

Arm positioning is another detail to be considered in all hugs. Where do your arms go? Do you go high, around someone's shoulders? Low around their waist? Or do you attempt a cross arm approach to a hug?

Once you've got your arms in place, there are also some other handy variations you can use to round out your perfect embrace.

The Over Arm Approach

The Over Arm technique involves wrapping your arms around the neck or shoulders of the person you're hugging. It is a safe approach: your intentions cannot be misread and there is no chance of hands straying or giving the wrong impression. This approach is most commonly used on strangers, parents and by taller huggers on most anyone they wrap their arms around.

This approach is always returned with the Under Arm Approach.

Under Arm Approach

The Under Arm Approach involves sliding your arms around the waist of the person you are hugging. It is a personal and more intimate form of embrace. It involves a level of familiarity between the two parties that transcends a first hug. With your arms around someone's torso, you have free access to all areas of their back, from the shoulders right down to the waist.

This approach is always returned with the Over Arm Approach.

THE CROSS ARM APPROACH

The Cross Arm Approach is a combination of the Over Arm and Under Arm approaches. Each hugger has one arm over the shoulder and one arm around the waist of their hugging partner. This is one of the most common and accommodating approaches to a Free Hug.

THE HIGH FIVE

You know this one! Contrary to popular opinion, a high five and its modern descendant – The Fist Bump – are perfectly acceptable substitutes for sharing a Hug.

Some people just don't much like physical contact.

Poor things.

Used to celebrate an achievement or during moments of excitement, elation and happiness. High Fives are common amongst kids and sports people, but are found just about anywhere and at any time.

THE PAT

You're all the way into a hug and then you feel it... a hand gently patting you on the back.

A pat on the back is a comforting thing. Parents pat their newborns on the back to comfort them. People pat each other on the back as a sign of sympathy. You could call those the "There, there" pats, imagining somebody saying it every time they pat you on the back.

When offering Free Hugs a pat on the back means something different – it's there to keep a hug quick. When somebody starts patting you, it's a sure sign they're ready to let go.

If you've ever watched a pro-wrestling match, you'll recognise the pat as a sign that someone wants out of the position they're in. Fast!

THE RUB

The Rub is a hand on your back, gently rubbing in circles.

This is another throwback to parents and babies. Parents rub their children's backs or limbs to calm them. A rub on the back is a nice way of soothing your pains or showing someone you care. It's also a great way to generate warmth on a cold day.

THE HEAD HOLD

Holding someone's head or touching their face is a wonderful sign of love in an embrace.

It shows a level of comfort, appreciation and respect for the person you're hugging.

THE HAND SHAKE

The Handshake is a hug tailor made for hands. Two people's hands are clasped together, with a shake for emphasis.

When people aren't too comfortable with the idea of hugging somebody, sometimes a handshake will suffice. It's a personal way of making contact with somebody in a way that isn't too physical or intrusive.

ADVANCED HUGGING TECHNIQUES

We've covered the anatomy of a hug and the way our bodies, arms and hands all contribute to the delivery of a great embrace.

There are some circumstances and situations that require a more advanced hugging technique for both parties.

These techniques aim to close the distance between two huggers so they may enjoy the benefits of a hug, regardless of the situations or circumstances that keep them apart.

These advanced hugging techniques are used in conjunction with the great variety of hug types, approaches and variations to deliver a tailor made hug.

THE SWAY

When engaged in any form of embrace, the huggers slowly and softly sway from side to side.

Gentle, rhythmic and romantic, it replicates the tender motion of a parent rocking a baby to sleep. If one hugger is swaying in a hug and the other hugger isn't aware that they too should be swaying, it can become a touch awkward.

THE TWIST

Two huggers are engaged in any kind of hug, with their feet placed firmly on the ground, their upper bodies twist from side to side, similar to the working of a pepper grinder.

This variation is most common among excited or enthusiastic people or people who may not have seen each other in some time.

THE BENDED KNEE HUG

The Bended Knee Hug is a great way to address the difference in height between two huggers. A hugger bends down on one knee and delivers a hug to the hugee utilising any of the previously mentioned hug styles and techniques.

Taller huggers, taking into consideration the height of children and smaller people, will on occasion get down on one knee and hug away!

At first, a Bended Knee Hug may seem awkward for both huggers. It brings attention to the height disparity between them. But no matter what height people may be, once they are caught up in an embrace, the details aren't as important as the hug itself.

THE LAZY HUG

Using any of the various different styles of hugs, a hugger initiates the Lazy Hug when they lean on and place all of their body weight upon the huggee.

A Lazy Hug can go wrong if the huggee fails to catch the weight of the hugger, or if they step away from the falling hugger. This is a hug of faith, as the hugger must have great faith in the huggee being there to catch their fall.

This is also an exhausted hug. At the end of a long day, a hugger may be inclined to collapse into the arms of somebody and hope that they'll be there to catch them when they fall.

THE ONLINE HUG

Four letters on a screen. A single word letting you know that somewhere, someone in the world is thinking about hugging you. All you need to do is type the word...

Hugs

People across the world use it every day, signing off on an email, leaving a message on someone's web page or slipping it into a text message. Why finish an email saying "Sincerely yours," when you can write "Hugs," and let your correspondent know you care?

Users of the Online Hug use technology as way of decreasing the distance between people. Laptops, cell phones or any new piece of electronic wizardry – one word that shows somebody you care, no matter how close or far away they may be.

This type of hug uses the technology that can keep us physically apart to close the emotional distance between us.

You can even kick it old school by writing it in a letter...if you know where to find stamps, envelopes and a mailbox – that is.

How to begin offering Free Hugs

We've covered the styles of hugs, the technique of hugging and some of the finer points of an embrace. Now how about we put that new found knowledge into practice? You can hug your family and your friends, so why not hug a stranger as well?

Starting your own Free Hugs Campaign is simple to do. All you need is yourself, something that has the words "Free Hugs" on it and a place filled with people ready to take you up on your offer!

Here is some friendly advice about starting your own Free Hugs Campaign:

Promoting Yourself and Your Free Hugs

Make a sign that says "Free Hugs" and carry it around for the day.

Design it however you like so that it can be easily read from a distance. Decorate it, colour it in, make it eye catching, attractive and most importantly - fun.

Make or buy a T-shirt that says "Free Hugs" and wear it anywhere.

But why buy a shirt when you can make your own? Remember, whenever you wear your Free Hugs shirt, wherever you are, someone will come up to you and ask for a hug, so be prepared!

After you've got your advertising covered, finding a place to offer Free Hugs takes a little consideration. You can walk down any street with your sign or shirt, but if you're the only person there, who is there to hug?

Selecting your Free Hugs Location

In choosing a place to offer Free Hugs it's a good idea to find a busy public place – parks, public squares or busy pedestrian areas. There are more prospective huggers walking around and for both the safety of you and others, it is important to stay on public property in busy areas.

Other great places to offer Free Hugs are festivals, major events and anywhere there are lots of people looking to enjoy life.

Inside private property like shopping malls, amusement parks and stores may not be such great places to offer Free Hugs and it is often a good idea to get permission in advance from the people in charge of these places.

For those looking to offer Free Hugs while at school or college – be prepared to have to argue your case with teachers and other staff.

Let them know you are trying to do something to make people smile, that to hug is to be human and you're doing it for charitable reasons. So charitable, it doesn't cost a single cent.

You might just find they'll let you offer Free Hugs until your arms are ready to fall off!

Offering Free Hugs

You have something that shows you are offering Free Hugs. You've chosen some places where you're going to offer these Free Hugs, now all you have to do is get out there! But what can you expect from people and what might people be expecting from you? Here are a few things I keep in mind every time I'm offering Free Hugs.

BE FRIENDLY - Stand around, wave and talk to curious bystanders. If someone's smiling, great! If they're frowning then wish them a great day as they walk by.

Do NOT HUG SOMEBODY UNLESS THEY OFFER TO HUG YOU - An unwanted, uninvited hug can be threatening and unwelcome. The purpose of the Free Hugs Campaign is to offer Free Hugs to those who want and need them, not to force yourself on those who might be scared, intimidated or uninterested.

WEAR COMFORTABLE CLOTHING - You really have to make sure you're comfortable if you're going to be standing around all day. In summer, not only will you be incredibly hot, by the end of the day you'll be incredibly sweaty. In winter you'll be battling the cold, so stay warm and rug up.

REMEMBER TO SMILE - Someone walking past may just smile and maybe double back for a quick hug. Even if they don't, they won't soon forget the happy people they've just seen offering Free Hugs!

WHEN HUGGING SOMEONE, BE MINDFUL OF THEIR PHYSICAL CONDITION - Don't pick up someone frail and twirl them around like you would a dancing partner! Unless they run and leap into your arms, a nice old fashioned hug is just fine.

WHEN THE PERSON YOU ARE HUGGING STOPS HUGGING YOU, LET GO - If they're patting you on the back, let go faster. Go with the flow and let the person you're hugging guide the hug.

OFFER FREE HUGS WITH A GROUP OF FRIENDS - It'll be a great experience that you'll all remember. You'll laugh together about the people you meet, cry over the stories you hear and when the crowds disappear and it's quiet again, you have someone to talk to.

WHEN OFFERING FREE HUGS IN GROUPS, REMEMBER TO KEEP YOURSELVES APPROACHABLE - Try to avoid standing around chatting with each other, otherwise people will think you're too busy to hug them and won't want to bother you. There is no need to scream 'FREE HUGS' at people passing by. If you're wearing a Free Hugs shirt or carrying a Free Hugs sign, they'll understand exactly what's on offer.

SOME PEOPLE DO NOT WANT A HUG - But they will settle for a handshake. Some people may just want someone to talk for a moment. Others may just wonder if you're crazy, if you're with a religious group, a university study or a TV program. Everyone, no matter how stern they look, is going to be curious about these happy looking people they see offering Free Hugs.

THE BENEFITS OF FREE HUGS

What's so great about Free Hugs anyway? So everyone's doing it, done it or plans on having one later on, why should you?

FREE HUGS:

FEEL GREAT – A Free Hugger is a hugging veteran. With many hugs worth of experience, they'll deliver a quality hug every time or your money back!

MAKE YOU FEEL LESS LONELY – A Free Hugger is someone who will try to understand. They are someone who will listen to you, laugh with you and cry with you.

GIVE YOU THE COURAGE TO DO ANYTHING – If you can share a Free Hug with a complete stranger, you can do absolutely anything you set your mind to.

CAN HELP YOU FEEL – When all the pain and sorrow in the world has you feeling numb, a Free Hug can help you find that spark that makes life worth living once again.

BOOST YOUR SELF ESTEEM – Knowing that there's somebody out there who wants a hug from you can help you feel better about yourself.

INSPIRE YOU TO MAKE A DIFFERENCE IN THE WORLD – If something as simple as a Free Hug can make a difference, what else could you do to make your part of the world a better place?

IMPROVE YOUR HEALTH – Happiness is one of the greatest boosters for your immune system you can get!

HELP YOU RELAX – A tough day at work? Problems at home? A Free Hug will ease that tension and help you remember that there are good people in the world.

ARE GREAT EXERCISE – If doing a hundred push ups is great for conditioning your muscles, walking around offering hundred Free Hugs can be of great benefit for you.

ARE COMPACT AND PORTABLE – You can take your Free Hugs sign or shirt with you and share them anywhere. Wherever you go a Free Hug can go with you!

REQUIRE NO SPECIAL TRAINING – We've all hugged someone before which means we're all experts. All you need to get started is something that tells people, "Hey, I'm offering you a Free Hug," like a T-shirt you've made or a sign you've created.

ARE A GREAT WAY TO CELEBRATE – The world is treating you well? Why not share that awesome feeling with someone else and offer them a Free Hug?

ARE ENDURING – Hours and even days after your Free Hug is over, just the thought of it will make you smile again. The effects can last for as long as you want them to!

COST NOTHING – It doesn't matter how much money you have, what clothes you're wearing, where your ancestors are from or what you believe in, you have nothing to lose and everything to gain from offering Free Hugs.

THE NEGATIVE ASPECTS OF FREE HUGS

Offering Free Hugs is an amazing experience. Your city will open its arms to you, some people will smile at you, others will wish you well and a few special people will thank you for the wonderful service you are providing. A larger number will throw themselves upon you and hug you as though you've never been hugged before.

Then when you're smiling and waving to an elderly man who's trotting down the street after having his first hug in years, it will happen.

Someone will squeeze your arse.

When offering Free Hugs you're putting your body on the line and there are a very few negative individuals out there who will take advantage. It doesn't matter if you're male or female, what clothes you wear or where you're offering Free Hugs.

If somebody has the audacity to grope you, confront them and tell them what they did is unacceptable. You aren't alone, you have your friends to support you and the general public will take your side!

Whatever you do, don't let one horrible person ruin the Free Hugs experience for you or anybody else. Remember, you're doing an amazing thing.

There's another negative aspect to offering Free Hugs.

Your face will hurt from smiling too much.

Mine always does.

FREE HUGS - A TRUE STORY...

Free Hugs. Two words and a gesture that changed my life. I have travelled around the world and seen people offering Free Hugs in the most unlikely countries. I have met more kind hearted people than I could ever have imagined. I have been welcomed as a guest into stranger's homes, shared a meal and a part of their lives.

I have seen old friends take the opportunity to chase their dreams and others drift away, while welcoming new friends into my life and into my home.

I've come a long way from that sad and lonely man standing in an airport longing for someone to hug him.

I've celebrated International Free Hugs Day, the first Saturday after June 30th, every year since I began offering Free Hugs in June 2004.

I've hugged hundreds of thousands of people from all over the world . Together, we have laughed, we have cried, we have hugged.

I have learned that the beautiful thing about life is knowing that I am the one that gets to put it my life together.

My Dad's words were a truth I came to terms with. I may not have changed the world but I have made a difference. Even if it's just in one person's life and in a simple way, like making them smile or offering them a hug.

The smallest gesture can have the greatest impact.

A smile from a stranger, a kind word from a friend, a thank you from a loved one. A hug from someone who cares. Alone, one person can make a difference. Together, we can change the world.

Tomorrow I'll wake up with the sun. I'll open my cupboard and take out my red velvet jacket. I'll pick up a piece of cardboard and a marker and make a sign that reads "Free Hugs."

Wherever in the world I may be, I will make my way into the city and I will wait there with arms wide open and a smile on my face.

Would you like a Free Hug?

Further Information

International Free Hugs Day is the first Saturday after June 30th every year.

For more information about Juan Mann and the Free Hugs Campaign check out the following websites:

The Official Home of Juan Mann

www.juanmann.com

www.facebook.com/juanmann

You can contact Juan Mann personally by emailing him:

juan@juanmann.com

For more work by the artist Krista Brennan check out her website:

www.kristabrennan.com.au

OUR MODELS

A very special thanks to the kind souls who posed for the illustrations that appear in this book.

Elana-Lee McIntyre, James Lawton, Susie Conway, Sean Bailey, Catherine Lin, Daney Faddoul, Margot Lichtenstein, Matthew Kermeen, Mee Yeon D'Arcy, Lucky Velasquez, Leah Roqueza, Clair Ross, Alissar Elias, Melissa Douglas, Anthony Newton, David Chandraratnam, Holly de Havilland, Stuart Roberts, James McPhee, Janice Guan, Michelle Brownlow, Nicola Jentner, Carolin Bader, Jessica Rizk, James Phillip Davies, Kyall Phillips, Sean McKenzie, Kathleen Alberto,Kayzen Clavano Kian Manalo, Christine Manalo, Olga Rozenfeld, Bojan Ristevski, Pavel Sosnovsky.

ACKNOWLEDGEMENTS

JUAN MANN WOULD LIKE TO THANK:

Mee Yeon D'Arcy, Russell Elsarky, Krista Brennan, Mitch Brown, Joe Gobeli, Holly De Havilland, Yonit Belnick, Bojan Ristevski, Pavel Sosnovsky, Eva Larumbe, Jenny Tomlinson, Tara Cook, Adam Dwyer, Casey Wallace, Leah Watson, Ruth Powell, Jon Turner, Olga Rozenfeld, Ben Amato, Kate Dolenec, Jessica Blacklock and the citizens of the City of Sydney. To everyone who tried to break me down and everyone who helped build me up on the way. I thank you.

KRISTA BRENNAN WOULD LIKE TO THANK:

Juan Mann, Mitch Brown, Mee Yeon D'Arcy, Pat, Lindy, Kalindi and Tulasi Brennan, Giovanna Aryafara, Nicky Howard, Shaun Wells, Rachel Austin, Paul Farmer and Ben Beard. Without the unswerving love, enthusiastic support, encouragement and generous empathy you've all shown me, I doubt I could have made it this far. Special thanks to David Briggs, Narin Kittisuwannadech, Andrew Paviour, Richard Porter, Sam Wade, Eric Wadsworth and the Julian Ashton Art School.

Printed in Great Britain
by Amazon

25382169R00046